THE FEUDING FAMILY
EVERYONE LOVES TO LAUGH AT

is back in a brand-new
cartoon collection of hilarious cracks
and humor-packed punch lines!

THE LOCKHORNS
in

*"I COULD LIVE
WITHOUT THESE
MEALS—
PROBABLY LONGER!"*

by
BILL HOEST

"I COULD LIVE WITHOUT THESE MEALS— PROBABLY LONGER!"

THE LOCKHORNS
by
BILL HOEST

A SIGNET BOOK

NEW AMERICAN LIBRARY

TIMES MIRROR

Ⓢ

SIGNET TRADEMARK REG. U.S. PAT. OFF. AND FOREIGN COUNTRIES
REGISTERED TRADEMARK—MARCA REGISTRADA
HECHO EN CHICAGO, U.S.A.

SIGNET, SIGNET CLASSICS, MENTOR, PLUME, MERIDIAN AND NAL
BOOKS are published by The New American Library, Inc.,
1633 Broadway, New York, New York 10019

First Printing, August, 1982

1 2 3 4 5 6 7 8 9

PRINTED IN THE UNITED STATES OF AMERICA

"I COULD LIVE WITHOUT THESE MEALS— PROBABLY LONGER!"

"CONGRATULATIONS, LEROY! MY WOMEN'S GROUP HAS UNANIMOUSLY VOTED YOU CHAUVINIST OF THE YEAR!"

"LORETTA'S BEEN PLAYING SINCE SHE WAS A LITTLE GIRL. NO ONE EVER HAD THE NERVE TO STOP HER."

"ONE REASON OUR MARRIAGE HAS LASTED SO LONG IS THAT HE'S SLEPT THROUGH MOST OF IT."

"ANOTHER SIX-PACK EVENING. WHAT ABOUT YOU?"

"THAT WAS THE SMOKE ALARM. DINNER SHOULD BE READY ANY MINUTE NOW."

"I DIDN'T SAY YOU WERE WRONG. I THOUGHT IT WAS OBVIOUS."

"WHAT ARE YOU WAITING FOR . . . CLEARANCE
FROM THE CONTROL TOWER?"

"THAT'S NOT FAIR, LEROY! I'VE ALWAYS BEEN THE
FIRST TO SAY YOU'RE RIGHT . . . BOTH TIMES!"

"FORGET YOU MENTIONED WHAT?"

"THAT WAS YOUR WIFE, MR. LOCKHORN. SHE SAYS
TO BE SURE TO WATCH THE ELEVEN O'CLOCK NEWS."

"I THINK I COULD BALANCE THE BUDGET IF YOU'D MOVE OUT."

"IT WAS A TYPICAL DOUBLE-RING CEREMONY. HE PUT ONE ON HER FINGER AND SHE PUT ONE THROUGH HIS NOSE."

"NO, ACTUALLY I HAD AN EASY DAY AT THE OFFICE.
IT WAS THE DRIVE HOME THAT DID ME IN."

"IT'S THE AMERICAN AUTOMOTIVE REPAIR
ASSOCIATION. THEY WANT TO HOLD AN
APPRECIATION DINNER FOR YOU."

"MY WIFE IS ONE IN A MILLION. AND I'D GLADLY TRADE HER FOR ANY OF THE OTHER NINE HUNDRED NINETY-NINE THOUSAND NINE HUNDRED NINETY-NINE!"

"LOOK AT IT THIS WAY, LORETTA. YOU HAVE A ROOF OVER YOUR HEAD, YOU'VE GOT SECURITY, NO MANDATORY RETIREMENT."

"I'LL ALWAYS HAVE A WARM SPOT FOR LORETTA'S MOTHER. SHE'S THE ONE WHO TRIED TO BREAK US UP."

"I KNOW I INSISTED ON COMING! NOW I INSIST ON GOING!"

"NO, I'M NOT JUDGING HER BY HER CLOTHES. THERE'S NOT ENOUGH EVIDENCE."

"AMAZING! BURNED TO A CRISP AND SOGGY AT THE
THE SAME TIME!"

"I DON'T MIND HER HAVING THE LAST WORD. I'M DELIGHTED WHEN SHE GETS TO IT!"

"I THINK I HEAR A BURGLAR GROANING DOWN BY YOUR REFRIGERATOR!"

"YOU SHOULDN'T COMPLAIN ABOUT THE COST OF LIVING. LEAVE THAT TO THE LIVING."

"WELL, YOU'RE OFF TO A GOOD START. YOU'RE NOT
LISTED IN THE OBITUARIES."

"DID YOU ARRANGE TO HAVE SOMEONE KEEP THE PHONE WARM WHILE WE'RE GONE?"

"YOU DON'T HAVE TO *AGREE* WITH HER ALL THE TIME, MR. LOCKHORN. JUST TRY TO SHOW SOME RESPECT FOR HER SILLY OPINIONS."

"DRESS UP ALL YOU WANT. I'M STILL NOT LEAVING
A TIP."

"SO, DO THE DISHES *WITHOUT* THE APRON IF IT RUINS YOUR MACHO IMAGE!"

"YOU'VE BEEN DRINKING FROM THIS SAME POT OF COFFEE FOR THREE DAYS AND NOW SUDDENLY YOU DECIDE YOU DON'T LIKE IT!"

"SHE'S THE ONLY LARGE MOUTH I EVER CAUGHT."

"THE LAST TIME LEROY WENT ON A DIET ALL HE LOST WAS HIS SENSE OF HUMOR."

"IT'S GRAVY . . . ONE LUMP OR TWO?"

"WELL, IF YOU DON'T WANT TO HELP ME FIND SEASHELLS, WHAT *DO* YOU WANT TO DO?"

"I WARN YOU! I'M GOING SHOPPING WHETHER YOU GET THE RAISE OR NOT!"

"ONE GOOD THING ABOUT YOUR COOKING . . . IT MAKES ME THIRSTY."

"THIS IS OUR RUMPUS ROOM . . . AND THERE'S THE RUMP."

"FRANKS AND BEANS AGAIN . . . YOU'RE SPOILING ME."

"NOW, ISN'T LOSING TO ME BETTER THAN LOSING TO THE TRACK?"

"HOW WOULD YOU LIKE TO HAVE THE LAST WORD
FOR ONCE IN YOUR LIFE?"

"BUT HOW CAN I OPEN DINNER WITH THE POWER OFF?"

"WHAT DID THE PLUMBER THINK OF YOUR SUGGESTION?"

"STOP TAILGATING, LEROY!"

"SHE'S BUSY RIGHT NOW, COMMITTING DINNER."

"WE'LL NOW HAVE WINDS GUSTING UP TO EIGHTY M.P.H."

"I COULD LIVE WITHOUT THESE MEALS . . .
PROBABLY LONGER."

"THEY ALWAYS LOOK SO LONELY WITHOUT MARTINIS AROUND THEM."

"YOU KNOW VERY WELL WHAT I MEAN WHEN I SAY, 'GET INTO YOUR EVENING CLOTHES'!"

"THE *NIGHT* MAY BE YOUNG BUT YOU'RE NOT."

"WELL, IT WAS WORTH A TRY, I GUESS . . . AT LEAST
YOU DON'T LOOK ANY WORSE."

"IT SAYS YOU ARE BEAUTIFUL, INTELLIGENT AND A GOURMET COOK. IT HAS YOUR WEIGHT WRONG, TOO."

"WAIT TILL YOU TRY LORETTA'S HALF-BAKED ALASKA."

"I KNOW SHE'S 'JUST A SWEET KID.' I ALSO KNOW YOU HAVE A SWEET TOOTH."

"I DON'T WANT YOU TO GIVE UP E.R.A., BUT WHY CAN'T YOU COMBINE IT WITH HOUSEHOLD DRUDGERY?"

"SAY, THAT'S A GREAT BEAUTY TREATMENT! YOU LOOK BETTER ALREADY!"

"YOU CHANGE THE SUBJECT SO OFTEN I HAVE NO IDEA WHAT WE'RE ARGUING ABOUT NOW."

"I HAVE NO TROUBLE DIETING IF I STICK STRICTLY TO LORETTA'S COOKING."

"ONE THING I'LL SAY FOR HER, MURRAY, SHE GIVES ME THE INCENTIVE TO GO TO THE OFFICE EVERY DAY."

"BUT YOU'RE *SUPPOSED* TO HAVE A HARD DAY AT THE OFFICE. IT'S THE AMERICAN WAY."

"HERE'S AN INTERESTING FACT, LEROY. A GORILLA SPENDS SEVENTY PERCENT OF HIS TIME SLEEPING."

"LEROY? THIS IS LORETTA . . . BETTER POUR
YOURSELF A STIFF DRINK . . ."

"I SEE THE SAP IS BEGINNING TO RUN."

"NO, IT'S NOT TOO BRIGHT . . . IT'S YOU."

"DR. PULLMAN NEVER GIVES UP. HE SAYS HE'LL RECONCILE US IF IT TAKES EVERY DOLLAR WE'VE GOT."

"IN THIS HOUSE 'HEALTH FOOD' IS ANY MEAL YOU LIVE THROUGH."

"... AND ANOTHER THING ..."

"THE DONUT IS BOUNCING OFF THE COFFEE."

"WHAT HAVE YOU DONE WITH MY WIFE, YOU FIEND!"

"NO, I DON'T HELP WITH THE HOUSEWORK. I'M MORE OF A CONSULTANT."

"DO YOU REALIZE THAT I PAY MORE IN TAXES NOW
THAN I EVER DREAMED ABOUT EARNING?"

"WHAT DO YOU MEAN, 'DON'T I LOVE YOU?' ARE YOU TRYING TO START ANOTHER FIGHT?"

"IF WE LIVED IN THE ICE AGE HE'D PROBABLY GET RUN OVER BY A GLACIER."

"DINNER TIME, EH? ALL RIGHT . . . I'M GAME!"

"LORETTA CAN'T OPEN HER MOUTH UNTIL SHE'S HAD HER FIRST CUP OF COFFEE . . . SO I HIDE THE COFFEE!"

"ALL I CAN SAY FOR LORETTA'S COOKING IS THAT IT'S CONSISTENT."

"NICE TRY."

"I HAVE SOME RELATIVES I'D LIKE YOU FOLKS TO MEET . . . I'LL SEND THEM RIGHT OVER."

"THE MERCHANTS' ASSOCIATION SENT YOU A GET-WELL CARD."

"I LIKE THE PART WHERE THE GUY SITTING IN BACK OF YOU KNOCKED YOUR HAT OFF."

"LORETTA'S NOT PUTTING IN A GARDEN THIS YEAR. LAST YEAR THE ONLY THING THAT GREW WAS THE WATER BILL."

"IT DOESN'T TASTE ONE BIT BETTER WHEN YOU BURN IT OUTDOORS."

"THAT WAS THE FIRST TIME I EVER BEAT MY HUSBAND AND I JUST WANT TO THANK YOU FOR BREAKING HIS CONCENTRATION."

"OLD FRED DID SOME SPRING CLEANING . . . GOT RID OF HIS WIFE."

"THANK GOODNESS YOU'RE HOME! WHERE HAVE YOU BEEN?"

"DON'T LOOK NOW . . . BUT LOOK WHO JUST CAME IN."

"OUTSIDE OF MY LITTLE EXTRAVAGANCES WHAT ELSE DO I SPEND MONEY ON?"

"SHE'LL BE READY TO TALK TO YOU IN A MINUTE, HELEN."

"LET'S MAKE THIS SNAPPY. I TEE OFF AT ELEVEN SHARP."

"IT'S BAD ENOUGH THAT WE LIVE A PERFECTLY
NORMAL LIFE, BUT YOU SEEM TO ENJOY IT!"

"JUST ONCE I'D LIKE TO ASK FOR A MEASLY FEW HUNDRED DOLLARS WITHOUT YOUR WANTING TO KNOW WHAT FOR!"

"THE LENHARTS SAY THEY'RE PICKING UP YOUR LEG OF LAMB ON THEIR TV SET!"

"LOOK AT IT THIS WAY, LEROY . . . YOUR HORSE IS LEADING THE SLOW GROUP."

"I WOULD HAVE BEEN A JUNE BRIDE, BUT LEROY'S
BACHELOR PARTY LASTED UNTIL JULY."

"TALK ABOUT NERVE! SOMEONE BROKE IN AND LEFT AN AD FOR A BURGLAR-ALARM SYSTEM!"

"DON'T ASK *HER* ABOUT INCOME. SHE'S DISBURSEMENT."

**"WHAT DO YOU MEAN TAKE OUT THE GARBAGE?
WHAT WAS THAT WE HAD FOR DINNER?"**

"I GOT ANOTHER DENT IN THE CAR. SEE IF YOU CAN FIND IT."

"WHO NEEDS STEREO? I HAVE A WIFE AND A MOTHER-IN-LAW!"

"WELL, I CAN SEE THEY TRIED."

"LEROY ALWAYS CELEBRATES THE FOURTH WITH A FIFTH."

"IT SOUNDS LIKE A FOOL'S PARADISE . . . AN IDEAL PLACE FOR MY HUSBAND."

"THE STEAK'S NOT A TOTAL LOSS. WE CAN TOAST
OUR MARSHMALLOWS ON IT."

"LEROY, WHAT WAS THAT I SAID THE OTHER DAY
THAT YOU THOUGHT WAS PROBABLY TRUE?"

"FOR WHAT IT'S WORTH, THAT CUTE BLONDE JOGGER WITH THE GORGEOUS FIGURE MOVED OUT OF TOWN YESTERDAY."

"WHAT DID YOU PUT IN THIS . . . THE EXTRA
CANDLES?"

"IS THAT SUPPER I SMELL OR ARE THEY
BLACK-TOPPING THE DRIVEWAY NEXT DOOR?"

"KNOW SOMETHING? THERE'S NOT ONE DROP OF MEDICINE IN THE MEDICINE CHEST."

"I'M GOING TO LOOK FOR A COAT. COULD I HAVE $399.99?"

"MY MARRIAGE IS LIKE THIS . . . IF I EVER SUE FOR DIVORCE, IT'LL BE IN THE SMALL CLAIMS COURT."

"SOMEONE PULLED THE WELCOME MAT OUT FROM UNDER HIM."

"OH, OH . . ."

"WHAT'S HAPPENING TO US? WE DON'T EVEN HATE THE SAME COMMERCIALS ANYMORE."

"WHAT WAS THAT YOU SAID THE OTHER NIGHT
THAT I SCOFFED AT AND YOU FOUND OUT LATER
WAS STUPID?"

"WE HAVE EVERYTHING MONEY CAN BUY. NOW WE'RE WORKING ON WAYS TO MEET THE MONTHLY PAYMENTS."

"TOO TART?"

"OF COURSE I'M SORRY TO SEE YOU GO LIKE THIS.
YOU'VE GOT MY LUGGAGE."

"I SUPPOSE I SHOULD GO HOME, BUT I HATE GOING ANYPLACE I'M NOT WANTED."

"YOU AND HER MOTHER ARE THE SAME AGE."

"I THOUGHT I'D BRING FRANK HOME FOR ONE OF YOUR DELICIOUS HOME-THAWED DINNERS."

"LEROY, WAKE UP! LONI ANDERSON WANTS YOU TO HELP FIND HER BIKINI SHE LOST ON OUR FRONT LAWN!"

"TELL THE HEAD OF THE HOUSEHOLD I'D LIKE TO HAVE A WORD WITH HER."

"IF IT'S REALLY SERIOUS, DOCTOR BLOG, I'LL ONLY
PLAY NINE HOLES."

"WITH LORETTA AROUND I NEVER HAVE TO WORRY
ABOUT AN AWKWARD LULL IN THE CONVERSATION."